SCHOOL SAFETY

Printed in the United States of America.

Library of Congress Cataloging-in-Publication Data
Loewen, Nancy, 1964-
School Safety/Nancy Loewen.
p.   cm.
Includes bibliographical references (p.).
Summary: Offers rules for behaving in a safe way in the classroom,
on the playground, and while waiting for and riding the bus.
ISBN 1-56766-255-2
1. Schools--Safety measures--Juvenile literature.
[1. Schools--Safety measures. 2. Safety.]
I. Title.
LB2864.5.L64 1996
371.7'7-dc20   95-25898
                                          CIP
                                          AC

SCHOOL SAFETY

By Nancy Loewen Illustrated by Penny Dann

THE CHILD'S WORLD

You probably spend a lot of time at school. In a way, going to school is your job! And like any job, you have **responsibilities**, such as listening to your teacher and doing your **assignments**. Pickles and Roy will show you what to do—and what not to do—to practice safety sense at school!

You are responsible for behaving in a safe way, whether you are in the classroom, on the playground, or riding the bus.

Wait for the school bus at your bus stop. Stay back until
the bus comes to a complete stop.

If you need to cross the street to reach the bus, wait for the driver's **signal** before crossing. Walk at least ten feet in front of the bus, so the driver can see you.

Enter the bus single file, and use the hand rail.

Stay in your seat when the bus is in motion. The driver needs to **concentrate** on bringing you to and from school safely, so don't do anything that might be **distracting**.

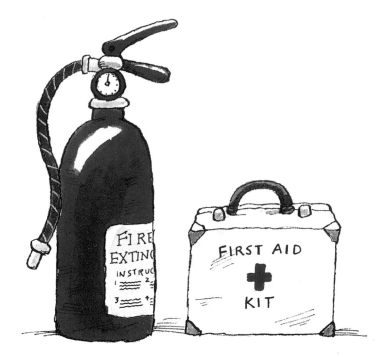

First aid kits, fire **extinguishers**, and other important safety tools are on the bus for emergencies. These tools need to be in working order at all times, so don't play with them. You never know when they'll be needed!

Stay seated until the bus comes to a complete stop.
Get off the bus in a single file, and move away from the
bus quickly.

Watch out for traffic when getting off the bus. Drivers don't always pay attention to the safety rules.

Walk, don't run, in the halls or on stairs.

Don't stand up on chairs, desks, or tables.

14

Handle scissors and other sharp objects with care. Put them away when they are not in use.

Don't play near drinking fountains or in rest rooms. If the floor gets wet, it also gets slippery, which could lead to falls.

16

During emergency drills, keep your voice low and listen carefully to instructions. If you do this you'll know what to do in a real emergency.

Respect crossing guards and playground patrols. They're working to keep you safe, and that's an important job!

18

On the playground, stay in the area chosen for your age group. Use the equipment the right way—don't try risky tricks.

Check to see that the area is clear before you swing, slide, or jump rope. And make sure that swings, merry-go-rounds, or other moving things have come to a stop before you get on or off.

Be especially careful on ladders and other climbing toys. Take a firm hold of the **rungs**, and don't climb higher than you can handle.

Treat others the way you would want to be treated.

Remember, you don't need to follow the leader—or the crowd—if they're doing dangerous things. Be a smart leader yourself and stay safe at school!

Glossary

assignments (e-SĬN-ments)
tasks to be done. Today's assignment in Math is on page 3, problems 1-5.

concentrate (KON-sen-trät)
pay close attention. The driver needs to concentrate on bringing you to and from school safely.

distracting (dis-TRAKT-ing)
confusing, disturbing. Don't do anything that might be distracting to the bus driver.

extinguishers (eks-TING-gwish-rs)
a small tank filled with chemicals, for putting out small fires. First aid kits, fire extinguishers, and other important safety tools are on the bus for emergencies.

responsibilities (re-SPON-se-BIL-e-ties)
duties, obligations. Like any job, you have responsibilities such as listening to your teacher and doing your assignments.

signal (SIG-nel)
sign giving notice of something. When you need to cross the street to reach the bus, wait for the driver's signal before crossing.

rungs (rungz)
a rod or bar forming a step of a ladder. When climbing on a slide, take a firm hold of the rungs.